how to grow
micro**greens**

how to grow microgreens

quick, easy ways to grow & eat nature's tasty superfoods

FIONNA HILL

F

FRANCES LINCOLN LIMITED
PUBLISHERS

For my friend Dorothy

Front cover Snow pea microgreens. SALLY TAGG/NEW ZEALAND GARDENER
Back cover Mustard microgreens. FIONNA HILL
Opposite title page Basil 'Sweet Genovese'.
Opposite A 'microgreen meal' (clockwise from back left): Radish sango, cress, snow peas, beetroot 'Bull's Blood'. SALLY TAGG/NEW ZEALAND GARDENER

Frances Lincoln Limited
www.franceslincoln.com

Microgreens
Text © Fionna Hill, 2010
Typographical design © David Bateman Ltd, 2010
Copyright to photographs remains with the contributors, please see Photo Credits page 99.
All other photographs © Fionna Hill, 2010

First published in 2010 by David Bateman Ltd,
30 Tarndale Grove, Albany, Auckland, New Zealand
www.batemanpublishing.co.nz

A catalogue record for this book is available from the British Library.

ISBN 978-0-7112-3471-0

1 2 3 4 5 6 7 8 9

Printed in China

contents

'Microgreens are maybe the oldest foods in the world. Our great, great ancestors knew why to eat them. We are just learning again.'
— *Rob Baan, Koppert Cress.*

Left: Harvesting pea microgreens 'Fiji Feathers' for lunch.
Opposite: Mustard microgreens in a hypertufa pot.

1

introduction: houseplants you can eat

'Just because you've only got houseplants doesn't mean you don't have the gardening spirit. I look upon myself as an indoor gardener.'
— *Sara Moss-Wolfe*

- What are microgreens?
- The benefits of growing your own
- Using microgreens

Remember growing cress in a saucer on the windowsill? Microgreens are an updated version of these home-grown mini-greens. The idea originated in the United States and microgreens have become the hottest new food and garnish in some of the world's finest restaurants. They are available commercially and are now appearing in family kitchens as home growers catch on to producing their own.

What are microgreens?

They are larger than sprouts and smaller than 'baby' salad greens (the small leafy greens, edible flowers and herbs that are popular salad ingredients). Microgreens are termed that after they have produced at least two 'true' leaves after the cotyledons appear. Cotyledons begin as part of the embryo within the seed of a plant. In dicotyledonous plants they produce two kidney-shaped 'seed' leaves, the first leaves to appear. True leaves, by contrast, develop from the plant stem.

MICROGREENS VS. SPROUTS

Microgreens are not the same as sprouts. There are several key differences.

Sprouts are basically germinated seeds. You eat the seed, root, stem and underdeveloped leaves. They are generally grown in dark, moist conditions.

Microgreens cannot be grown using these methods; they are planted and grown in soil or a soil substitute, and the seed concentration is a fraction of what is used in sprout growing. After the initial germination period, usually a day or two, microgreen seedlings are grown on in high light conditions with normal humidity and good air circulation.

If the stem is cut, leaving the roots behind, and it is not grown in water, it is a microgreen, not a sprout. Also, microgreens have much stronger flavours than sprouts, with a wide range of leaf shapes, textures and colours.

Above left: Pea and wheat seeds at the sprouting stage ready to be grown on as microgreens.
Above right: Kale microgreens.
Left: Italian parsley microgreens.

Above left: Fenugreek planted in a recycled and painted food can that has had drainage holes punched in the bottom.
Above right: Mustard growing in seed-raising mix in an empty egg shell.

The benefits of growing your own

Nutritious microgreens are today's popular gourmet garnish and flavour accent, offering a multitude of colours, textures and distinct flavours. For a few years now, they have been in commercial production for home consumers to buy. Greens available have differed from country to country, but popular products have included mustard, cress, snow pea shoots and wheatgrass for juicing. Microgreens are now appearing at farmers' markets and some quality fresh-food stores.

The problem with bought greens, however, is that they may have been boxed and shrink-wrapped, put in cold storage or transported long distances before they get to the retailer. To be able to pick your own, wash them and toss them straight into a salad is very appealing.

Fresh is best

Growing microgreens allows the production of high-quality, risk-free food. The leaves have high nutritional and biological values. Grown at home, they are harvested immediately before their use and so are fresh, with their nutritional and medicinal qualities intact.

They keep well in the fridge, but they have more goodness freshly picked. And another benefit of home-growing: you only need to pick the required amount.

Colour, texture, flavour, variety, versatility

Microgreens will add punchy splashes of colour, texture and many flavours to dishes ranging from spicy and hot to mild and subtle. Pea shoots taste just like freshly picked garden peas. And radish leaves taste like radish flesh. Some are grown for their attractive appearance, texture and colour, while others are sought after for their flavour and aroma. Some provide both. They're immediate and practical. Most are ready in a week or so and you can grow them in winter.

Microgreens are a way of making a striking and healthy salad by adding to shop-bought greens or serving alone. They have many more uses than salads, too. The seedlings add flavour, colour and texture when included in sandwiches, used as a garnish, or mixed into soups, dressings, meat dishes, pies, dips, stir-fries, pizzas and breads, or decoration on a platter of canapés.

Full of goodness

Nutritionally, microgreens pack a powerful punch; they're full of dietary goodness like vitamins, minerals and enzymes. They are at their nutritional and flavoursome best when they begin to display the adult-shaped leaves. Microgreens have been found to contain higher levels of concentrated active compounds than found in mature plants or seeds (see Nutrition chapter, page 39).

These tiny baby plants provide a convenient and concentrated means for absorbing the active compounds when made into a health drink, as is commonly done with wheatgrass.

Cheap and fun

I began allotment gardening a few years ago after my introduction to microgreens and I can now make interesting dishes with ingredients that have been growing only hours or even minutes before I prepare them. Micros will grow indoors too. The investment is low compared to what you would pay for them at retail prices and they require very little previous knowledge. Growing them yourself is the cheapest option, not to mention a lot of fun.

Small-scale and natural

It doesn't take much space to grow microgreens. They can be grown in the smallest of apartments, and in the densest of cities. They are small-scale and make sense for a single person or a couple, but you can grow them in volume according to how many mouths you are feeding. The concept of saving space and having something

*Above: Mixed, growing microgreens for sale
in a farmers' market.*
Right: Broccoli microgreens.

so fresh and available is ideal in an urban setting. They look attractive too.

For those with limited garden space or, like me, in a second floor apartment, microgreens are great to grow in containers on a terrace or small outdoor space. Containers on a small balcony adjoining my kitchen are my 'garden'.

Also, for me, they connect me to the natural world while I'm living in the centre of a large, sterile city. Putting my hands in soil, planting seeds and nurturing them to grow connect me to the earth and to my food. And my spirit is nourished as well as my body.

Using microgreens

My first taste of microgreens was bought for me by my sister Shirley at a farmers' market. I was hooked. Since then I have been experimenting with them and am enjoying mixing and matching my crops and learning about their nutritional qualities.

At the beginning of my experimentation, in my enthusiasm I planted too many at once and ended up with enough greens to feed my whole apartment block! Trial and error is the key.

Above: Raw energy salad with red microgreens – red cabbage, purple basil and radish. See recipe page 85.
Left: Radish sango.

Flavours

Some microgreen crops can be left to grow up to four true leaves. Microgreen seed is grown at high density so that seedlings grow tall and straight. Their flavour is intense and varies for different vegetables and herbs as it does with sprouts and salad greens.

Flavours also change as the plant grows. As the leaves open, they begin to manufacture energy from light. That gives them a change in flavour. The most intense flavour comes when that first leaf opens.

Many microgreens are grown specifically for their distinctive flavour, that is sometimes more subtle and delicate than the mature plant. Other spicy and pungent greens may be combined with lesser flavoured types of salad greens or used on their own as an important ingredient of a dish.

It's up to the person doing the eating, of course, to determine what they like, sharp or mild. My favourites are radish, rocket (arugula) and mustard streaks, but I'm still experimenting. In the garden, I have lots of failures with rocket and basil as full-grown herbs, but not so with them as microgreens. Basil is slow but the end result is splendid and surprisingly good with strawberries (see recipe page 96). As I'm a little heavy handed

Above: Chick pea and zucchini salad with mustard and fenugreek microgreens. The spicy microgreens are a good foil for the mild flavour of the vegetables.

with their fine seeds, I sometimes have dense mounds of these two gorgeous greens.

I use micros in dishes such as flans, or with comfort foods. Gooey egg sandwiches with a touch of onion, mayo, and masses of cress and mustard microgreens. A cosy baked potato popped open and served with a generous dollop of crème fraîche, ground pepper, capers and a heap of broccoli and garlic chive microgreens is delicious.

Growing and harvesting

Grown in soil or soil-like materials, microgreens depend on sunlight and air circulation to flourish. Cut just above the soil, microgreens are harvested when 2 to 5 cm (¾ to 2 inches) tall and seven to 21 days old when their very first leaves appear. Their short growing time makes them ideal for summer when you may be more likely to be away or occupied with other activities. You have more control and need less commitment than for a vegetable garden.

This book highlights 25 microgreen crops or varieties. They provide different textures, flavours, shapes and sizes. There's no need to try everything. Like me, find your favourites.

2

growing microgreens

'Plants give us oxygen for the lungs and for the soul.'
— *Linda Solegato*

- Seeds
- Containers
- Soil or other growing media
- Sowing the seeds
- Covering
- Watering and plant nutrition
- Locations to grow
- Plant care
- Harvesting, cleaning and storing

Seeds

All microgreen seed should be untreated. Buy seed from a reputable source. If possible, use seed that has been produced and packaged specifically for microgreen or sprout growing. This should mean that the seed has a low percentage of 'foreign matter' or contamination from other species and is clean and high quality. Seed treated with fungicide should be avoided as it risks contamination because fungicide or other chemicals can be carried over to the harvestable portion of the seedling. Peas and spinach often have fungicide-treated seeds for garden growing.

Also, some countries, such as New Zealand, Canada and Australia, require that some varieties of edible seed be heat-treated, thus making them impossible to sprout.

Organic microgreen seed is available although it can be higher in price than non-organic seed. Some companies sell both organic and inorganic seed. I buy both

Top row, left to right: Kale, flax, snow peas, beetroot 'Bull's Blood'.
Centre row, left to right: Mung beans, peas 'Fiji Feathers', rocket (arugula), radish sango.
Bottom row, left to right: Italian parsley, garlic chives, wheatgrass, cress.

organic and non-organic seeds from the same company. Seeds are normally purchased by weight and should be stored in an airtight container. Microgreen seeds are sold in bulk and my supplier sells a choice of several quantities. Buy small quantities at first so that you can experiment and find favourites.

It's difficult to measure the volume of greens you can expect from seeds but there's no doubt that they're better value than buying fresh cut microgreens. They are also economical to grow because they deliver large yields.

Weight varies considerably from variety to variety depending on the day of harvest and the water content of the micros. It's interesting to note that the pea variety 'Fiji Feathers' is the same weight at 7.5 cm (3 inches) long as it is when 10 cm (4 inches) long.

Containers

I choose containers that look attractive because they are on two balconies that are seen from my kitchen and I want to enjoy them aesthetically as well as nutritionally. Microgreens promote the use of recycled materials, thus making low-cost materials such as wood and disposable containers useful.

Fenugreek microgreens in a bonsai bowl. Microgreens don't need a lot of soil or pumice to grow well, and a wide, shallow dish maximizes the growing area.

Shallow, lightweight, portable

Having containers that are shallow, lightweight and portable is the key. They could be recycled plastic food trays or food cans; old baking pans with holes punched in the bottom are good, too. Shallow with holes in the base for drainage is the rule.

There's no need to have masses of soil or pumice. If you already have large pots that you'd like to use, they are fine but there will be unnecessary soil use. Wide and shallow is better than deep and tall so that the growing surface area is maximized. (Peas, however, will send down long roots so the growing medium becomes thick and matted and will not be able to be used again; they do not require a deep container for success.)

Drainage is vital

Remember that all containers need drainage; it's one of the keys for a plant to succeed. Lack of drainage will mean that you may have mould, rot and undersized growth. If you put containers inside more aesthetically pleasing holders (such as the example on page 69) they are good for watering; they hold water while the plants drink, but be sure not to leave them for a long time with their feet in water.

Hygiene needs to be considered, too. Ideally, germination containers should be cleaned with bleach between crops.

Above: Wheatgrass has been planted in plastic seedling pots then slipped inside cardboard noodle boxes for fun single helpings.
Left: Wooden trug planted directly with seed-raising mix and radish sango.

Planter possibilities

Old mushroom boxes are ideal, if not aesthetically pleasing. Shallow baskets can be lined with plastic film such as polythene/polyethylene (garden supply outlets sell tough polythene by the metre/yard) or shallow plastic trays can be put inside them. The tiny wooden trug above made a lovely gift full of growing greens but the basket trug, which was unlined, will eventually deteriorate.

Recycled large food cans can be painted, too, although some hold more soil than is necessary. Small food cans are good for children to experiment with; flat sardine cans are perfect. All cans will need some holes punched in the bottom. Our small can on page 79 fits inside a large plastic vinegar bottle with its lid removed; this creates a mini glasshouse and keeps bird thieves at bay.

Low-priced, shallow plastic seed-raising trays from garden supply outlets are excellent; they are good for families who need bulk micros. Some nurseries have used trays that would otherwise be thrown out. These may be too large for household use; several smaller pots are better for this purpose.

Terracotta, although it looks appealing, will dry out quickly. It has a tendency to dry and take moisture from the soil so can impede germination. You could line terracotta with plastic but make sure to create a drainage hole. Plastic is durable but may not be ecologically smart. Terracotta bulb bowls are shallow with drainage; I painted mine for fun.

My favourite containers are shallow pottery bonsai planters that I buy from an Asian supermarket. I also use bamboo steam baskets that can be bought from

Asian stores; they have drainage in the bottom and look lovely. They are also designed to get wet. I use their lids with a damp kitchen towel underneath to begin the germination process.

I sell growing micros in a farmers' market and for that purpose use shallow plastic fast-food containers with a drainage crack punched in the bottom, or recycled, rectangular plastic seedling pots from a garden supply outlet. These are portable for shoppers and provide small quantities of greens for family purposes. They are good for children's experiments or solo diners.

Pallet planter

For those with available space or room in a glasshouse, a wooden pallet can be used. Use a pallet measuring approximately a metre (yard) square and create sides by nailing or screwing planks 15 cm (6 inches) wide to the pallet's edges. Line with old fleece, fill with multi-purpose compost and press it down. Then measure out equal-sized intervals along all sides and use pieces of doweling or thin bamboo to run across the top of the compost to create a grid pattern. This will create over 50 squares. One whole planter like this allows for easy, even watering.

Sow different seeds in the squares at time intervals. You could thin out your seedlings of microgreens and leave some to grow into baby leaves (they need about 2 cm (¾ inch) square for each baby seedling as salad greens). Alternatively, eat a whole square as microgreens. Pull out the leaf stems and roots and plant another crop. Sow little and often — say every two weeks for a continuous supply.

Growing in the ground

Of course, you can plant microgreens in your garden or, even better, in raised garden planters outdoors. They're not as easy to cut at or near ground level, however, as bowls can be lifted to a convenient height on a bench or table to harvest.

Right: Although microgreens are ideal for growing indoors in containers they can be planted directly into the garden.

Above: Red clover seed just planted in seed-raising mix and fennel seed in pumice.
Left: Using seed-raising mix to plant tiny plastic scoops of microgreens for individual helpings.

Soil or other growing media

Edible shoots are tender young seedlings so they require a growing medium that will hold and transfer sufficient moisture and oxygen around the seed without waterlogging or drying out frequently. Microgreen growers have utilized materials as diverse as paper towels, burlap sheets, perlite, vermiculite, rockwool and specialized microgreen mats for this purpose, although loose media can create problems with grit particles contaminating the harvested product.

My experience is with both seed-raising mix and pumice and my advice reflects this.

Seed-raising mix

With seed-raising mix I cut the stems as it is difficult to clean soil off tiny uprooted greens. Seed-raising and potting mixes vary in quality. Go for high grade and look for additional ingredients like kelp and shellfish meal. This way you will have strong, even growth and a higher yield. Experiment with different brands — you may be surprised at the differences in outcome.

Pumice

Pumice is clean and I can harvest greens by pulling them out and often can eat the whole plant, roots and all. However, the light pumice may be raised up by the growing stems so you need to remove these particles. Some garden supply outlets sell ground, sterilized pumice specifically for potting and hydroponics. Hydroponics is the science of growing plants using a solution of suitable nutrients instead of soil. In conventional gardening the plants are grown in soil and take their nourishment from the chemical compounds within that soil. The hydroponic gardener replaces the soil with a balanced, nutrient-rich solution that the plant can absorb with ease.

Pumice is part of the hydroponic system known as 'aggregate culture'. Other materials that are in this category are sand, gravel and marbles. These media support the plant roots. It is important to note that the support material, unlike soil, does not absorb nutrients. It merely traps it in the spaces between the grains or stones, allowing the plant roots to freely take up the liquid. Pumice is porous and has excellent retention of air and water that's necessary for a healthy plant — roots need to breathe, too!

Pumice has proven to be an effective medium for me. I also use seed-raising mix but find pumice is cleaner, especially in a small apartment environment. I can pull the microgreens out cleanly with roots and all, and no wad of soil remains on the tips. Then I wash them and chop the roots off. I still use seed-raising mix for tiny seeds such as basil as these tend to drop down between the pumice 'stones'. And I am still experimenting.

HYDROPONICS

In Latin, the word hydroponics means 'water working'. Hydroponics is a way of growing plants in nutrient-enriched water instead of soil, thus eliminating any bacteria and impurities from the soil.

In soil, organic matter breaks down into nutrient salts that plants feed on. Water dissolves these salts and allows uptake by the roots. For a plant to receive a well-balanced diet, everything in the soil must be in perfect balance. Such ideal conditions are rare in soil.

With hydroponics, water is enriched with these same nutrient salts, creating a nutrient solution that is perfectly balanced. And because this solution is contained, it does not harm our environment as does runoff from fertilized soil. Also, in a hydroponic system very little water is lost to evaporation.

Pumice is often used to support the plants in a hydroponic system, as it is porous and has excellent retention of air and water that's necessary for a healthy plant.

As well as receiving a perfectly balanced diet, hydroponic plants have their food and water delivered directly to their roots. This way, the energy normally used to develop long roots can be redirected to growing more leafy matter. It's organic, environmentally responsible, sustainable and safe. Microgreens are well-suited to hydroponic production.

Sowing the seeds

Consider growth rates

Planting several types of seeds in one container can be tricky, as all seeds do not have the same growing time. If you're trying to grow a blend of microgreens, remember that different plants grow at different rates. For example, herbs grow slowly while radishes grow quickly.

Sometimes there are unexpected outcomes for no apparent reason. You need to gain some experience in how fast these crops grow from seed to harvest. Some are ready in eight to 10 days but others may take as long as three weeks.

Other factors include the time of year, the location (indoors or out), temperature and light. If I want the classic combo of mustard and cress I plant cress first; it takes longer. However, I find it better to plant separate crops in separate containers and mix and match after harvesting.

Pre-soaking

Larger seeds such as peas, corn and wheatgrass may be pre-soaked. Place in warm water and leave for 24 hours before planting. Not all growers carry out this step. Some microgreen seed is mucilaginous, meaning that once it is wetted it will form a thick gelatine-like layer that holds moisture. Cress is one of these and should not be pre-soaked before sowing.

Above left: Wheat and pea seeds soaking overnight to make germination quicker.
Above right: Wheat and pea seeds after one day's growing.

Above: Fenugreek seed planted on pumice in a small Asian bamboo steam basket.

Add growing medium

Fill your chosen containers with the growing medium that you've chosen:
4 cm (1½ inches) of soil depth is sufficient. Don't fill containers right to the top as
seed may spill over the edges when you water. Level out the soil and flatten down
gently. Over-compaction will slow growth down and results will be poor.

Sow seeds

Sprinkle seeds evenly over the surface. A small pinch of seeds in the fingers,
as if you were hand-sprinkling pepper on a meal, is a good way. If you get some over-
generous areas just spread out the excess.

The density depends on the size and type of seed you've chosen. For a dense crop
that you can harvest at cotyledon stage, plant a thick layer of seed. Be careful, however,
not to sow so many that they grow poorly and rot, or too sparsely and produce a low
yield. Alternatively, if you want to grow on to a larger 'true leaf' stage, sow less densely,
and let them grow for longer. I sometimes pinch out a bunch of cotyledon stage
seedlings for my first serving and leave the remainder to grow true leaves.

Give the planted tray a light pressing to settle your seed in the soil but not too firm
so as to compact it. This encourages your seeds to easily set roots.

I try to time it so that I have some microgreens ready to harvest, a quantity that is
germinating and a batch I am sowing. This is not as easy as it sounds — there are
many factors at play.

Above left: Micro seeds with damp paper kitchen towels and shower hat coverings to keep in the moisture.
Above right: Micro seeds in plastic punnets of seed-raising mix with damp paper towels.

Covering

Soil layer

Seeds need a covering layer to keep them warm and moist until they germinate. (They do not need light in order to germinate.) For tiny seeds such as kale, mustard and basil it should be a fine layer of sifted soil to the depth of the sowed seed (but not pumice — this is too lumpy). Make sure the seed is covered. A kitchen strainer (like a pasta strainer) works well to sift the soil. Large seeds such as pea and beet don't need sifted soil. After covering the tray, give the seeds a gentle press down. If watering exposes some seeds, sprinkle a little more soil over the top.

Cloth or paper towels

Rather than covering freshly planted seeds with soil, my preferred option is to use cloth or paper towels as an effective and clean alternative. I use light, old, linen or cotton tea towels or unbleached, natural paper kitchen towels. Lay them directly onto the seeds and dampen. These create a moisture blanket. Keep the towel moist until the seeds have germinated. This method also allows you to lift the fabric or paper corner to check on progress.

Wash the fabric towels often between uses as wet towels can build up bacteria and mould. Avoid fabric with looped pile. I tried fine cotton washcloths but found that many seeds entwined their way through the loops and were pulled up when I raised the cloth to look.

Give your seeds a generous watering. Under-watering will result in poor or no germination. Keep the seed moist all the time. If you allow them to dry out, they may not germinate.

Covers

Your containers will now need to be covered. This helps speed up germination and growth by holding in heat and moisture. It creates a mini-greenhouse effect. It means a more consistent environment for the seeds, especially if the growing space is subject to wind and the change in night and day temperatures.

Watch out for too much moisture and potential for mould. Keep an eye on them, too, if they receive direct sunlight, to make sure that the atmosphere inside is not too hot and steamy — they don't need a sauna.

Clear plastic is a good cover. I use light, clear plastic shower caps to put over the small cloth and container. Food covers with elasticated edges are also ideal. A pane of glass is also suitable, but not in direct sun as the heat becomes excessive.

Horticultural supply stores, garden supply outlets or nurseries sell clear plastic lids. Or check online.

Above: A damp cloth cover has been used since planting for these just-germinated seeds. It could be used for another day, but take care to keep an eye on the seeds at this stage, especially if you are in a warm, humid environment, as they can become mouldy very quickly. Also, avoid fabric with looped pile that the tiny sharp shoots can weave their way into.

Watering and plant nutrition
Nutrient needs

Microgreens are different from sprouts in their nutritional requirements and like a dilute nutrient solution to be applied to maintain foliage quality and growth rates. Sprouts are typically soaked and misted with only water because the seed contains sufficient reserves for the short period of time these are grown. Microgreens, however, are grown to the point of developing their first true leaves or sometimes even longer, and therefore need some diluted nutrient solution to support this process.

Initially, microgreen seed needs to be germinated in water only; any salts applied at this stage can cause germination problems.

Once the cotyledons are visible and starting to develop chlorophyll, the seedling will have exhausted the reserves contained in the seed. At this stage, the young plant is starting to photosynthesize, and nutrient ions will be absorbed by the root system.

A very shallow seed-raising mix will give plants some nutrition in the 14 or so days before harvest. Additionally, or if using a non-soil medium such as pumice, apply a general purpose vegetative or seedling nutrient formulation at the stated rates.

Water quality

The water supply needs to be of high quality as water can carry human and plant pathogens which may contaminate a crop.

Household water is fine for watering; a municipal water supply is treated to prevent the risk of contamination from

Above: These newly germinated seeds are past the covering stage. They are growing in pumice and ready for a general purpose vegetative or seedling nutrient formula. They will, however, grow with water only and look and taste good, but won't have the nutritional content that you may prefer.

human and plant pathogens. In order to ensure the purity of the final product, it is essential that only drinking water or clean rainwater are used.

Maintain moisture

Maintain moisture constantly as your seeds grow. If you use a fabric cover and it is moist, so will the seed below it be. Keep seeds covered until they have germinated. They will begin to lift the towel or if planted densely in soil may lift the soil. That's OK.

Containers with soil will dry out more quickly than towels; they may need watering twice a day. Soil will be rinsed from the seeds as you water. This will prevent the seeds from becoming pale and puny.

Some seeds, such as radish, develop white fuzz on their stems. Don't be alarmed; it's a natural part of the root-setting process, not mould.

Above: Daikon radish planted in a shallow plastic takeaway container with holes punched in the bottom and then placed inside a kitchen bowl. Note how attractive it looks when it has grown on, see page 71.

Locations to grow
Some light and warmth

It is interesting to note that microgreens have much higher concentrations of vitamin C and health-promoting phytochemicals when grown in the light, compared to sprouts, which are typically grown in the dark.

As mentioned, the microgreen germination process does not require light but, once germinated, like most other plants, they need light to grow. Indoor gardeners with a sunny windowsill or balcony can take advantage of even the tiniest of spaces to produce healthy, fresh microgreens year round.

Light for shoot production doesn't need to be intense; young seedlings need much less light than mature plants meaning that these greens can be grown near a window. You're only germinating them to the first leaf. They are at their nutritional and flavourful best when they begin to display adult-size leaves. That can be done anywhere you can grab a little indirect sunlight.

And some warmth too. I live in a warm coastal climate without extremes of

Above: Microgreens really are great for small spaces and making the most of your container garden. In this terracotta container a young seedling of 'Blood Vein' sorrel has plenty of space around it to grow a small crop of basil microgreens.

temperature. During summer the mean daily temperature is 23°C (74°F) and in winter 14°C (57°F). For germination, ideal temperatures range from 12.7 to 24°C (55 to 75°F). However, different crops have different requirements. Your seed packet should provide guidance.

Ideal for small spaces

Microgreens are ideal for food production in urban and suburban areas. They offer the advantage of using places that have not previously been considered appropriate for food production — courtyards, small gardens, walls, balconies, rooftops.

My microgreen trays are placed on layered French metal antique plant stands on a tiny outdoor balcony adjoining my kitchen so I can see lots of plants at different levels when I look out. I grow herbs there, too, so some of the pots are generously massed. The overall look is lush and it hides the ugly traffic. Sadly, they are above a busy city road but that's where I live — so be it.

This is my 'kitchen garden'; I can take a few steps and pick a handful of fresh greens immediately before I need them. I'm much more likely to do this than walk to a glasshouse or outdoor space some distance away. However, having said that, I also have a vegetable allotment nearby.

Above: Mustard streaks (at back), radish sango and Daikon radish (right foreground) growing happily in containers on a window ledge.

Plant care

Once seeds have germinated, they need light to grow and flourish. Remove the towel and plastic lid. I sometimes keep the shower hats on to thwart the sparrows, but keep an eye out for too much moisture inside the plastic.

The greens will need to remain in light for seven to 14 days, depending on type; for example, rocket (arugula) grows fast and basil grows slow. They also need to remain moist; test this by poking your finger down the edge of the pot. Don't overwater or leave pots standing with their feet in water and don't water in midday heat.

Harvesting, cleaning and storing
Harvesting

Try to harvest microgreens just before you need them, but preferably not in the heat of the day. They are best harvested early in the day when the foliage is coolest. This will prolong the shelf life. Even in the shade on a hot day, they are likely to wilt and turn to mush if picked at that time. If this has happened, try soaking in cold water, but it may be too late. Nutrients begin to be lost as soon as the greens are cut so cutting at a cool part of the day is ideal, although not always possible. Pick just enough and leave the rest to continue growing. Edible shoots contain many

Above: Ready to harvest. A great crop of rocket (arugula) microgreens that has been planted in a standard clay trough.
Opposite: Snow peas partly harvested. They have been cut leaving shoots at the base for a second crop.

vitamins, including vitamin C or ascorbic acid, the levels of which are known to decline the longer the greens are stored after harvest.

Long-bladed sharp scissors are the best for harvesting; snip as if you were giving a haircut, holding sections loosely while cutting. Unless you are cutting above the cotyledons, the plants will not grow again. Sharp scissors will prevent excessive tissue bruising and crushing of the stems, which also reduces the greens' shelf life. Because microgreens are so tender at this stage, harvesters need to take particular care not to crush the delicate stems or foliage during this process.

Some species are more difficult to harvest than others, due to soft, light or feathery foliage; dill, fennel and cress are some of the softer varieties that need careful handling.

Cleaning

Washing may be unnecessary. Or sometimes just a quick rinse before serving is fine. If using pumice, the greens are less likely to need washing. If grown in soil, they are likely to need a rinse. If you've used the towel-covering method, less or no washing will be needed. Use cold water and a plastic tub that fits under the running tap to wash them in. Keep an eye out for rotten leaves, seed hulls and soil. These should wash off or float to the top and can be skimmed off; a bit tedious but necessary. Rest the greens on a dry towel and pat gently.

Storing

Microgreens are young and tender and therefore have a high rate of respiration and potentially a short shelf life if not stored and handled correctly. If refrigerated, microgreens should have a shelf life of three to four days and up to one week. However, basil microgreens need careful handling because basil is prone to chilling damage at cold temperatures, with foliage discolouring and blackening resulting from cool storage. Basil microgreens need the same storage conditions as mature cut basil, at temperatures above 4°C (40°F). Zip-lock plastic bags are good for storing greens as are reusable plastic containers with fitting lids.

3

solving plant problems

'Don't blame the seed if it fails to show – give it a second chance.'
— *Joy Larkcom*

- Seeds that do not germinate
- Seeds sticking to the covering towel
- White fuzz and mould
- Uneven germination
- Rot
- Drawn up and weak stems
- Yellow and underdeveloped leaves
- Burning
- Wilting after picking

Seeds that do not germinate

Use seeds that are not past their recommended growing date.

Has the stored seed become hot or wet? If the stored seeds have become too hot or wet the germination may be affected.

Are you growing in a suitable temperature? For example, amaranth and basil need warm constant temperatures.

If your strike rate is low, have you sown the seed densely enough?

Have you allowed enough time for them to germinate?

Under-watering can be a factor in the germinating process. The covering towel must remain damp so that the seed will remain damp. However, do not overwater; before the seed has set roots it is not essential for the entire container to be soaked; the top layer is the focus at this stage.

Extreme heat or cold can be a factor in germination. As mentioned, ideal temperatures range from 12.7 to 24°C (55 to 75°F), although different crops have different requirements. Check the seed packet or with the supplier.

I have had failures and not fathomed the reason. However, an advantage of growing such small crops is that any investment in cost, time, space and energy is small. I try again and change any variables that I suspect may be the cause. Trial and error is worthwhile.

Seeds sticking to the covering towel

If you want to check on the progress of your seeds, lift up just the corner of the paper towel rather than the whole lot. If the seeds and their roots are sticking to the towel it's too soon to remove it.

An encouraging sign to note is your paper towel lifting off the soil because the seedlings are pushing it up. If this is happening, they are ready to see the light and show their first leaves. It will disadvantage your seedlings to leave the towel on after that. They'll become tall and weak and more susceptible to rotting and tangling.

You will get the hang of it after a few attempts.

White fuzz and mould

You may notice white fuzz around the roots of seedlings. Radish often develops this and it is often mistaken for mould. It's not; it's a normal part of the germination process. It will disappear once the container is watered.

However, mould can turn up if the weather is cold, humid or wet for long periods. To recognize the difference, fuzz is light and spiky and surrounds the roots, whereas mould covers bare soil or surrounds the seeds and is fluffy looking. I've noticed basil is susceptible to mould.

It's not easy to control your environment; try moving the greens to a warmer area, or if you have noticed mould, uncover the seeds, water lightly, and move to an area with more light and circulating air.

Uneven germination

There could be several reasons for patchy germination. Have you sown the seed evenly? It's important to sow slowly and focus on even spreading.

The quality of the growing media or uneven mixing of it by the manufacturer can also affect the evenness of germination.

The place where your container is placed for germination may be a factor. Is part of it in the direct sun and part in some shade? A shady spot is best when germinating.

Some batches of seed may have patchy germination and germinate at different times. Regardless, I still grow and eat them. I'm not trying to sell them to fussy buyers, but, having said that, it's visually satisfying to see a solid, even carpet of tiny leaves.

Rot

One reason for rot may be too much water and too little sunlight. In summer heat and sun, watering once in the early morning and again in the evening should work well. But if the weather is cold, this regime of watering could set up rotting patches. Watering once in the morning is probably enough.

Municipal water supplies usually contain chlorine, which plants dislike. Drinking-water filters remedy this. The pH level (acidity/alkalinity) of the soil or medium is another factor. However, I do not go there — mine is a kitchen garden, not a science lab. Generally, seed-raising soil products have the correct balance.

Drawn up and weak stems

Light is the factor here. I grew some microgreens in a potting shed with moderate light and no direct sun. They became tall and spindly and paler in colour but were perfectly edible.

A growing area that gets full to partial sun for most of the day is ideal. My balcony does not have sun all day; it also can get strong winds. However, I do not choose to move my containers about following the sun; I have nowhere else to put them so I sometimes suffer the consequences. But I have lots of success, too.

Yellow and underdeveloped leaves

This condition is probably due to lack of nutrients in the growing medium. The quality of the growing medium or uneven mixing of it by the manufacturer could affect the evenness of germination. I have experimented with a low-cost seed-raising mix and a high-quality organic mix and appear to have more success with the more costly organic one. Lesser quality soils don't have the range of nutrients to maintain growth. Water pH can also be a problem; however, I've made my view clear on that.

Burning

Strong sun may burn leaves. Aesthetically, they're altered and also their reliability is weakened. Don't water in the heat of the day. If the plants around the edge of your container appear burnt, this may be because the edges have dried out first. Cut off the plants with burnt edges so that at least you can rescue the rest of your crop.

Wilting after picking

Wash cut microgreens in cool water as soon as possible after cutting. Use a sealed container to store them in the fridge. They can last up to a week. But for home growers it's not necessary to pick and store them; they can be used immediately.

4

nutrition

'At home I serve the kind of food I know the story behind.'
— *Michael Pollan*

- Functional foods
- Factors affecting nutritional value
- Super micro foods
- A healthy pastime

Functional foods

'Functional foods' is the newly coined name for food products that contain particular health-promoting or disease-preventing properties that are additional to their normal nutritional values. Microgreens are in this group and so demand for them is growing rapidly.

Microgreens also have been found to contain higher levels of concentrated active compounds than found in mature plants or seeds. Principal physiologist Tim O'Hare, of Australia's Gatton Research Station, said studies showed that, generally, the chemo-protective potential of some plant compounds is most concentrated in seeds and sprouted seeds but declines with growth, suggesting extra benefit from microgreens over fully grown plants.

Microgreens provide a concentrated, convenient method for absorbing the active compounds when made into a health drink, as is commonly done with wheatgrass, or used in other ways as our recipes show (see Chapter 7).

Factors affecting nutritional value

Microgreens are at their nutritional and flavourful best when they begin to display adult-size leaves. They have much higher concentrations of vitamin C and health-promoting phytochemicals when grown in the light, compared to sprouts, which are typically grown in the dark.

Produce nutrition is also affected by the quality of the media it is grown in, its harvesting method, its treatment after harvest, and how long it takes to reach your plate.

Vegetables start to break down as soon as they are harvested, not to mention the stress of packing and transportation and the temperature at which they are being held. The temperature determines the speed at which they lose their nutrients. This particularly applies to perishable greens.

Microgreens grown at home can be harvested immediately before you eat them, preferably with sharp scissors in the coolest part of the day to keep the nutrition intact. And they allow year-round access to fresh greens, even in winter. They're a fraction of the price of microgreens in stores. Also you can cut to suit your needs and leave the remaining microgreens to continue growing.

Super micro foods

Wheatgrass is the most well-known microgreen that is grown for its healthy compounds and properties. It's used as a supplement after juicing. Wheatgrass is believed to lower blood pressure and cholesterol levels, increase red blood cells, relieve blood-sugar disorders such as diabetes, and aid in the prevention of some cancers.

Other species such as flax, broccoli, red radish and red brassica also have researched health-promoting qualities. There have been many studies showing the link between cancer prevention and the consumption of brassicas (also known as cruciferous vegetables) such as broccoli, cabbage, mustard, rocket (arugula) and kale.

Phytoestrogens (also known as isoflavones) are a group of chemicals found in plants that can act like the hormone oestrogen, and may play a role in preventing certain cancers and regulating hormonal changes. They are commonly found in beans/legumes, soy beans (and so very prevalent in Asian diets), cereal brans, flaxseeds, and alfalfa and clover. Sprouts and microgreen alfalfa and clover contain high concentrations.

Broccoli microgreens

Broccoli microgreens are one of the 'health heroes'. They contain a micronutrient, a chemical called sulphoraphane (sulforaphane), that shows effective anti-cancer, anti-diabetic and anti-microbial properties. It is thought to kill the bacteria responsible for most stomach cancers and ulcers.

Jed Fahey (a nutritional biochemist in the Lewis B. and Dorothy Cullman Cancer Chemoprotection Centre at the Johns Hopkins University School of Medicine, Baltimore, Maryland) said, after a small, pilot study of 50 people in Japan, that broccoli microgreens, if eaten regularly, 'might potentially have an effect on the cause of a lot of gastric problems and perhaps even ultimately help prevent stomach cancer'.

Young broccoli has been shown to have up to 20 to 50 times as much sulphoraphane as fully grown broccoli.

Left: Mustard microgreens, as with other brassicas, such as broccoli and cabbage, have great health-promoting properties.
Below left: Broccoli microgreens – the 'health heroes'.
Below right: Red clover micros contain high concentrations of phytoestrogens.

Along with providing possible protection against cancer, a regular intake of sulphoraphane in young broccoli has also been shown to help prevent a range of other conditions including ulcers and arthritis, as well as high blood pressure, cardiovascular disease and stroke.

Broccoli microgreens and sprouts are the first and only products with a guaranteed amount of sulphoraphane glucosinolate (SGS), a naturally occurring antioxidant compound in broccoli. (Antioxidants are linked with the prevention of cancer and coronary heart disease.) Researchers at Johns Hopkins University believe that the presence of many phytochemicals including sulphoraphane may help explain why diets rich in fruits and cruciferous vegetables are associated with good health.

Low-fat diets rich in fruit and vegetables (such as broccoli microgreens), including vitamin C and fibre, may help reduce the risk of certain cancers. Hopkins researchers are attempting to confirm the role that SGS may have in this process.

Other brassicas

A study of the cancer-preventing potential of Asian and Western vegetables belonging to the brassica family has rated radish, daikon (Japanese white radish) and broccoli sprouts as the most powerful brassica-based anti-cancer foods, with the radish sprouts possibly outperforming broccoli sprouts. Darker coloured varieties are high in vitamins, minerals and antioxidants. Cabbage contains diindolylmethane, a compound that provides hormonal balance and is also a preventative for cardiovascular disease and may have properties to fight some types of cancer.

Flax seeds

Flax (linseed flax seed) seeds contain high levels of lignans and Omega-3 fatty acids. Lignans may benefit the heart and possess anti-cancer properties. Studies performed on mice found reduced growth in specific types of tumours. Flax may also lessen the severity of diabetes by stabilizing blood-sugar levels. According to the US National Cancer Institute, lignans are a member of a group of substances found in plants that have shown anti-cancer effects.

A healthy pastime

Other microgreens possess healthful properties; for example, research has shown basil's anti-inflammatory, antibacterial and antioxidant effects.

However, the health of our spirit is worth remembering, too. Planning and creating a microgreen garden are positive experiences. Planting seed, tending the plants as they grow, and enjoying eating the fresh produce of your own labour nourishes your spirit as well as your body. Gardens enhance our environment aesthetically, and it is fun and satisfying to watch the plants grow.

5

individual crops

'To own a bit of ground, to scratch it with a hoe, to plant seeds and watch their renewal of life — this is the commonest delight of the race, the most satisfactory thing a man can do.'

— *Charles Dudley Warner*

- Amaranth ('Mekong Red')
- Basil ('Sweet Genovese', 'Dark Opal')
- Beet ('Bright Yellow', 'Bull's Blood')
- Broccoli
- Cabbage (red cabbage)
- Chives (garlic chives)
- Clover (red clover)
- Corn (popcorn)
- Cress
- Fennel
- Fenugreek
- Flax (linseed flax seed)
- Kale ('Red Russian')
- Mizuna ('Red Coral')
- Mustard (mustard streaks, black mustard)
- Parsley (Italian parsley)
- Peas (snow peas, 'Fiji Feathers')
- Radish (green radish; daikon radish)
- Rocket (arugula)
- Wheatgrass

I have experimented with a range of vegetables and herbs that are suitable to grow as microgreens. There are many more possibilities, and the choices available differ from country to country, as well as the names the plants go by. If you wish to experiment with more, choose leafy crops such as spinach and collards, not fruiting crops like tomatoes. Herbs are good ones to try, although they take a long time to germinate.

I've chosen the following selection as they cover a range of flavours, textures, shapes, colours and nutritional values.

Have a look at the selections available in your country. (See the Resources, page 98.) You may need to do a little investigative work to decide what to choose.

Buy seed preferably that is intended as microgreen seed and that has not been treated for garden planting. Microgreen seeds are usually sold in bulk rather than in tiny seed packets (see page 17).

Amaranth

Amaranth 'Mekong Red' (*Amaranthus tricolor* 'Mekong Red')

Amaranth (also known as Chinese spinach) is traditionally grown as a grain in dry climates and has been described as a 'super grain', and 'the grain crop of the future'. The leaves of this attractive microgreen are a beautiful magenta colour and add a vibrant splash of colour and a tangy, sweet flavour rather than much weight to salads; they are very light.

The seeds prefer heat and consistent temperatures for germination, above a minimum of 20°C (68°F). Avoid growing amaranth in winter; it is best as a summer crop. Temperature fluctuations result in low or slow germination in addition to poor growth.

Amaranth traditionally grows as a grain crop in dry climates, so don't constantly saturate the soil. I have more success with this crop in seed-raising mix than in pumice, as the seed is tiny and falls between the pumice pebbles. The towel cover method is probably a good one for this crop too. It is fast growing and can be cut and left to grow again.

The microgreen leaves can be cut at cotyledon stage or left to grow on to true leaves when it will have a different texture.

Amaranth is native to the Americas and was a staple grain of the early civilizations of Central and South America. The Greeks noticed the long-lasting qualities of the flowers and revered them as a symbol of immortality.

In China and Vietnam the young seedlings are uprooted, washed, chopped and briefly steamed. In Singapore the stems are peeled and eaten like asparagus. In the US thinnings are eaten with collard and other greens. The Greeks boil the leaves and discard the water, which contains oxalic acid that is toxic if taken in excess. In South Africa and Namibia it's added to mealie meal (maize porridge).

Opposite: Amaranth 'Mekong Red'

Basil

A tender, low-growing herb, much featured in Italian and South-East Asian cuisines, basil is originally native to Iran, India and other tropical regions of Asia, and has been in cultivation for over 5000 years.

Basil used to be considered a royal plant; only the sovereign could cut it — with a golden sickle. There was also a time when it was almost compulsory in the decoration of cobbler's workshops.

Scientific studies have established that compounds in basil oil have potent

Above: Basil grown almost to the baby leaf stage.
Opposite: Basil 'Sweet Genovese'.

anti-inflammatory, antioxidant, anti-cancer, anti-viral, and anti-microbial properties. Basil also contains flavonoids that offer protection at a cellular level.

Basil 'Sweet Genovese' (*Ocimum basilicum* 'Sweet Genovese')

'Sweet Genovese' is the standard, most commonly grown variety of basil. Microgreen basil has a more subtle taste than the full-grown garden plant — it's lemony and luscious. A lovely addition to salads and soups, it's also good with desserts. Try a pinch with stewed fruit, or in a tomato juice cocktail. It's refreshing with strawberries and orange juice; see our recipe for Strawberries with Basil Microgreens on page 94.

Basil requires a steady, warm environment. It's a summer herb, and doesn't like great fluctuations in temperature. This can be a problem when the temperature drops at night. I've had many failures when the weather has changed quickly or temperatures are too low and inconsistent. The seed germinates readily at temperatures between 24 and 29°C (75 and 85°F). My seed turns alarming blue when it is first wet!

Basil grows low to the surface. If you've grown it in soil take care not to gather the soil up when cutting. Try to cut just before needed and don't wash it if possible. The greens are delicate and bruise easily. If you need to wash it, do so just before serving. Don't wash and store in the fridge; it will discolour or go black as does mature cut basil.

Basil 'Dark Opal' (*Ocimum basilicum* 'Dark Opal')

This is ornamental basil with dark purple seedlings. It's great for adding colour to a summer salad. It has a classic sweet basil aroma and adds rich flavour to a micro mix. It requires the same growing conditions as 'Sweet Genovese'.

Beet (*Beta vulgaris*)

Beet is a plant in the amaranth family, with numerous cultivated varieties, the most well known of which is probably the root vegetable known as beetroot or garden beet. Other cultivated varieties include the leaf vegetables chard and spinach beet, as well as the root vegetable sugar beet.

Beet cultivation, especially of leaf beets, dates back to 2000 years BC in the Middle East, Mediterranean, India and later in China and Europe. Beets are known to possess antioxidant properties; they are rich in vitamins B1, B2 and A.

There are many varieties and cultivars available, with availability of seeds and the names they are known by differing from country to country.

Beet 'Bright Yellow' (*Beta vulgaris* var. *cicla* 'Bright Yellow')

Beta vulgaris var. *cicla* is the leaf beet known as chard, also called Swiss chard, silverbeet, perpetual spinach, spinach beet, crab beet, seakale beet and mangold. It is the same species as the root beets, but plant propagators have accentuated the different parts of beet plants: chard/silverbeet has been allowed to grow broad leaves, whereas with beetroot the root has been accentuated.

These seedlings of 'Bright Yellow' have a beautiful yellow stem and deep green leaves. They make a lovely addition to a micro mix.

Soak the beet seeds for 24 hours to help with the germination rate and speed. I chose seed-raising mix rather than pumice so that the large beet seeds could be covered more easily. Some larger pumice pebbles can also weigh down the light seeds.

Make sure the large seed is covered with a kitchen towel and kept moist. Adding a teaspoon of liquid kelp to the water is a benefit. For best germination keep the beet at a steady temperature. After germination avoid keeping the soil too moist. Overwatering will result in rotting.

If the seed hulls are still attached, wait for a few more days to harvest. If some hulls remain they can be gently pulled off before harvesting or will come off in the washing process. Cut the stems close to the soil; the bright stems are a feature.

Beetroot 'Bull's Blood' (*Beta vulgaris* var. *crassa* 'Bull's Blood')

'Bull's Blood' is a popular seller as a choice for beetroot microgreens. It's an American heirloom. The seedlings are an intense purplish red colour on even very young seedlings, which means they enhance a green salad mix or provide a lovely accent in any mix. They have a slightly earthy flavour, reminiscent to that of a beetroot root. The earthy taste is due to particular microbial life in the soil that produces an organic compound called geosmin.

It's an ideal edible garnish for entrées, sandwiches, soups and stews. To store, refrigerate in a sealed container. For quality and flavour, use promptly.

Right: Beetroot 'Bull's Blood'.
Below: Beet 'Bright Yellow'.

Cultivation is the same as for Beet 'Bright Yellow' above. Soak the beetroot seeds for 24 hours to help with the germination rate and speed. Seed-raising mix rather than pumice means the large beet seeds can be covered.

Ensure the large seed is covered with a kitchen towel and kept moist. For best germination keep the beet at a steady temperature. After germination avoid having the soil too moist. Overwatering will result in rotting.

If the seed hulls are still attached, wait for a few more days to harvest. If some hulls remain they can be gently pulled off before harvesting or will come off in the washing process. Cut the stems close to the soil; the bright stems are a feature.

The Romans cultivated beetroot and used its leaves as a vegetable. They also used it medicinally for fever and constipation. In Russian cookery both the roots and leaves are used a great deal, particularly for soups.

Broccoli (*Brassica oleracea* var. *italica*)

'I like broccoli microgreens, I eat them all the time, but not every day.
Variety is the spice of life: I eat blueberries on the other days.'
— Jed Fahey of Johns Hopkins University

Another of the brassicas family, broccoli microgreens are easy to grow — in fact, one of the easier ones. Various hybrids and cultivars are available. Sow the seeds thickly to obtain heavy yields. When harvesting, cut high up so as to have an equal proportion of leaf to stem. If allowed to grow to the true leaf stage it can be woody. The greens are delicious; their flavour is distinctly that of full grown broccoli; some say cabbage. As with most other microgreens they're good in a salad and they're also lovely in the stuffed mushrooms on page 86.

As a health-giving vegetable, broccoli is hailed as one of the 'superfoods'. It is low in fat and high in dietary fibre, and rich in iron, minerals and vitamins A and C. Recently, it has hit the headlines for its researched anti-viral, anti-bacterial and anti-cancer properties (some of which were discussed in Chapter 4 on Nutrition). In particular, it is indicated as playing a possible role in the prevention of stomach cancer.

There have been many studies showing the link between cancer prevention and the consumption of brassicas such as broccoli, cabbage, rocket (arugula) and kale. 'We know that a dose of a couple ounces a day of broccoli sprouts is enough to elevate the body's protective enzymes,' says Jed Fahey of Johns Hopkins University. 'That is the mechanism by which we think a lot of the chemoprotective effects are occurring.' Broccoli has the same health benefits grown as a microgreen as grown as a sprout.

Broccoli originated from wild cabbage, native to parts of Europe. The Italians enjoyed it before the rest of the world. Catherine de Medici, who married the heir to the French throne, and Marie de Medici, the bride of Henry IV, both introduced Italian-style cooking to France along with such vegetables as broccoli, artichokes and Savoy cabbages.

Opposite: Broccoli.

Cabbage

Another of the brassica family, cabbages are now available in many colours, sizes and shapes. The cultivated cabbage is derived from a leafy plant native to the Mediterranean, common on sea coasts. It was known to the ancient Greeks and Romans, and was common in Europe during the first millennium AD.

High in vitamin C, cabbage also contains diindolylmethane, which provides hormonal balance and is also a preventative for cardiovascular disease and may have properties to fight some types of cancer. Apparently, it's good for hangovers, too (well, the Romans thought so).

Red cabbage (*Brassica oleracea* var. *capitata f. rubra*)

This form of cabbage has dark red or purple leaves, although the plant changes colour in response to soil alkalinity. There are many cultivars to choose from, such as 'Purple Head', 'Hardora', 'Mammoth Red Rock', 'Red Rookie' and 'Ruby Ball', although what is available differs from country to country.

Red cabbage has a mild cabbage flavour, attractive colour, red veins and purple stems. The seed germinates rapidly and is easy to grow. If you are using a glasshouse keep an eye out for marauding caterpillars. You may need a screen for egg-laying butterflies.

Don't leave red cabbage growing for too long as it loses its colour. Also, when harvested young it has a sweeter flavour and a more tender texture. It's easy to harvest and wash provided there is no rot in your crop. Seed hulls can be hard to spot as they are disguised by the dark purple colour.

Mix it with the magenta colour of amaranth and yellow beet. It's stunning. I love a cabbage combination, too: kale, broccoli and red cabbage.

Left: Red cabbage.

Above: Garlic chives.

Chives

Chives are the smallest member of the onion family, and are native to Asia, Europe and North America. They are rich in vitamins A and C, calcium and iron. They also reduce cholesterol, reinforce the immune system and have good antiseptic properties.

Garlic chives (*Allium tuberosum*)

Garlic chives microgreens are decorative and often used to replace mature chopped chive spears. The seeds are slower to germinate than other microgreens. The greens are great to use in salads, meat and fish dishes, soups and omelettes.

For best results, shallow sow seed at very high density and keep evenly warm and moist. Harvest by cutting with scissors at four to six weeks when approximately 5 cm (2 inches) high. After cutting, my chives grew again.

They have a rich garlic flavour. In volume they are tiny but make up for that in flavour. They may also be called rock chives and originated in the mountains of China.

Above: Red clover.

Clover

Clover is a legume, part of the pea family and related to alfalfa. Several clover species are cultivated as fodder plants for animals, including white clover and red clover. The plant grows freely and abundantly; the grass is palatable and nutritious.

Red clover (*Trifolium pratense*)

Sow the seed densely in seed-raising mix. I've sometimes found it may have a great initial burst of growth before it begins to rot slowly. Don't be too heavy-handed with the watering can, especially when watering from above. The plants are dense so it is easy to set up a too-humid environment.

Red clover has a crisp texture and a mild, nutty flavour. I like it in salads, sandwiches and wraps with other microgreens. Its true leaves are beautiful, resembling a minute lotus leaf on fine, delicate stems.

It provides big-time nutrition. Red clover has been a valued medicine since ancient times and was particularly valued for treating respiratory problems, colds, flus and infections in the nineteenth century. It contains phytoestrogens, common in the Asian diet (from soy products), and thought to be the reason why Asian men have lower incidence of prostate cancer. It is also a great source of essential oils, amino acids, vitamins and minerals that relax the nervous system and settle the stomach.

Corn

Corn and maize are basically the same thing. In most English-speaking countries, 'corn' is often used in culinary contexts, particularly when referring to products such as popcorn, but 'maize' is generally used in agriculture and science.

Maize was domesticated from a grass in ancient Central America, and spread throughout the American continents. After European contact in the late 15th and early 16th centuries, maize spread to the rest of the world.

Popcorn (*Zea mays* var. *everta*)

Microgreens can be grown from popcorn (just the kind you buy for popping), of which there are many varieties available. The large corn seed may be pre-soaked in warm water for 24 hours before sowing.

Above: Corn as a microgreen.

I've had success with both pumice and seed-raising mix as the growing medium. The shoots must be blanched to prevent them from turning green; I use a plastic bucket inverted over the top of the round microgreen planter and keep it on all the time except when watering. The resulting bright yellow shoots are sensitive to light and once cut need to be stored in closed dark containers to protect their vibrant colour.

The greens have an intriguing taste and visual appeal — an attractive yellow colour — and are highly decorative. They are extremely sweet and tender with a slightly sour aftertaste. They remind me of mild fresh 'sweetcorn' kernels.

Blanched popcorn micros need to be eaten very young, otherwise they get fibrous too quickly.

Use them in salads, and as a garnish use them quite prominently on the plate because the colour is like no other you have ever seen.

Cress (*Lepidium sativum*)

Cress is one of the oldest types of tiny greens. Do you remember growing cress on wet blotting paper on a saucer? Cress is a herb related to watercress and mustard, and shares their peppery, tangy flavour and aroma.

Both cress and mustard are easy to grow as a microgreen crop. They are perhaps the oldest types of microgreen grown: both have been harvested as a seedlings partnership for use in sandwiches and salads for many years.

Cress has small, tender, green seedlings on a white stem; they're fragile, so take care when harvesting and washing them. It has a piquant peppery flavour and is good to spike a salad, makes good herb butter, and is lovely as a garnish. Mixed with mustard it creates 'mustard and cress', seen often in England. It's traditional and yummy in gooey egg sandwiches with some mayonnaise and plenty of freshly ground black pepper. It's also an easy one to grow so it's a good one to get children interested.

If you would like to have 'mustard and cress', sow cress four days earlier than mustard so that the cotyledons or seedlings are ready at the same time.

Cress is known by a number of names, including common garden cress and peppergrass. A fast-growing, often weedy native of western Asia and Europe, it is widely grown, especially in its curl-leaved form, and the seedlings are used as a garnish.

Below: Cress.

Above: Fennel.

Fennel (*Foeniculum vulgare*)

Soak the fennel seed first and plant densely on top of seed-raising mix. It takes around 10 days before the greens are ready to cut. If left longer to grow with some true leaves, the plants are feathery and attractive.

Like fully grown garden fennel this microgreen is aromatic and has a liquorice or aniseed taste. It's less pungent than dill —sweeter and more aromatic. It's great as a palate cleanser. It has good digestive and diuretic properties, stimulating the appetite and relieving indigestion.

Fennel is of Italian origin (its Italian name is finocchio) and it has been grown for thousands of years as a culinary herb. It was known to the old civilizations of China, India and Egypt.

Several cultivated varieties are available. In the full grown plant, the seeds, leaves, flower heads and bulbous stems are all eaten. The Romans ate the young shoots as a vegetable.

It's good on pasta or pizza; add some to a serving of yoghurt to eat after spicy food or toss into a salad. It's good too in the Feta and Fennel Spread with Turkish Rolls (page 90).

Above: Fenugreek.

Fenugreek (*Trigonella foenum-graecum*)

Fenugreek microgreens are easy to grow albeit a little slow; they take around four weeks to microgreen-ready stage. I have always had success with them. Don't sow the seed too thickly as the plants are prolific.

The greens have light-green leaves, lovely white stems, a bittersweet flavour and a succulent texture. I add them to mixed green salads that include bland flavours such as that of lettuce. My Indian chemist suggests mixing fenugreek leaves with drained fresh cucumber into plain yoghurt with salt and pepper. Or making a salad of fenugreek leaves, a drizzle of oil and pinch of chilli.

The microgreens can be eaten raw or cooked. There is a traditional Malaysian fish soup with fenugreek sprouts, cellophane noodles (which are made from the starch of green mung beans), and the fish sauce nam pla.

A member of the bean family, fenugreek is cultivated worldwide as a herb and a spice (the seed). The sprouts are nutritious, particularly for women, and you can use them as a natural digestive aid. Fenugreek sprouts are rich in vitamins E, C, B and A, zinc, potassium, phosphorus, magnesium, iron, calcium, carotene, phytonutrients, chlorophyll, amino acids and protein.

Fenugreek seed is a characteristic ingredient in some curries and chutneys and is used to make imitation maple syrup. In India young fenugreek plants are used as a potherb. The young leaves and sprouts of fenugreek are eaten as greens and the fresh or dried leaves are used to flavour other dishes.

It is one of the oldest culinary and medicinal plants. In Yemen it is the main condiment and an ingredient added to the national dish called *saltah*. The similarity in the Arabic word *hulba* and Mandarin Chinese word *hu lu ba* indicate the significance of fenugreek in history. Fenugreek is also one of four herbs used for the Iranian recipe *ghormeh sabzi*.

Above: Flax.

Flax

Flax is also known as common flax and linseed, and is native to the region from the Mediterranean to India. (New Zealand flax, Phormium species, is not related to this flax.) Flax has been used as a fibre for over 20,000 years and more recently as a decorative plant. For culinary purposes, however, it is the seeds and the oil they produce that are important.

Linseed flax seed (*Linum usitatissimum*)

Because of its mucilaginous nature when germinating, flax seed is best grown and cut as a microgreen rather than as a sprout. It makes a gooey mess before rotting if you try to sprout it in a jar.

The seed comes in two basic varieties: brown and yellow/golden. Either can be used. Shallow sow the seed. Given some dirt to cover it or to adhere to, it makes a fantastic microgreen that can be snipped off at 5 cm (2 inches) tall. Cut in six to eight days at first leaf stage and store in the fridge for up to a week.

The leaves have a slightly spicy flavour. I add them to salads.

Opposite: Kale.

Linseed flax seed is highly nutritious and yields beneficial levels of vitamins, minerals and antioxidants. It also has high levels of lignans and amino acids including Omega-3. Lignans may benefit the heart and possess anti-cancer properties. Flax may also lessen the severity of diabetes by stabilizing blood-sugar levels.

As an alternative to the microgreens, use the seed itself (provided it has been bought for eating purposes) in a healthy morning smoothie combining yoghurt, milk, fresh fruit and one dessertspoon of flax seed per person. Blend and serve.

Flax microgreens may have slightly less nutritional value than flaxseeds put in a blender and added to smoothies, but to eat the flax microgreen on a regular basis is a good way of getting greens and omega-3 in one hit.

Kale

Kale is a leafy green or purple vegetable, another of the brassica family. Unlike cabbage, its central leaves don't form a head.

Until the end of the Middle Ages kale was one of the most common green vegetables in Europe. Curly-leaved varieties of cabbage already existed along with flat-leafed varieties in Greece in the fourth century BC. These forms, which were referred to by the Romans as Sabellian kale, are considered to be the ancestors of modern kales.

During the Second World War cultivation of kale in the UK was encouraged by the 'Dig for Victory' campaign. The vegetable was easy to grow and provided important nutrients to supplement those missing from a normal diet because of food rationing.

Kale 'Red Russian' (*Brassica oleracea acephala* 'Red Russian')

Kale microgreens grown in warmer temperatures are a beautiful grey/green shade. In cool temperatures their stems have a super purplish red hue and their green colour is enhanced. This variety is a traditional one that's lovely in the vegetable garden, too.

It's surprisingly subtly sweet, tender and succulent, with finely cut, wavy leaves. In colour it teams well with bright yellow and magenta microgreens such as yellow beet and amaranth. Salads are my favourite way to use it. Or it's a colourful addition to dishes such as rice paper rolls (page 82) or Turkish rolls (page 90).

It's easy to grow and is a good winter microgreen.

Brassicas have gained recent widespread attention due to their health-promoting properties (see Chapter 4, Nutrition). As well as phytonutrients, kale is high in beta carotene, vitamin K and calcium.

Above: Mizuna 'Red Coral'

Mizuna

Mizuna is the Japanese name for two species of mustard greens: *Brassica rapa* and *Brassica juncea*. It is known by various names, including Japanese mustard, Japanese greens and California peppergrass. There are over a dozen varieties available. Mizuna has been cultivated since ancient times in Japan, although it probably originated in China. The plants contain vitamin C, folic acid and antioxidants. Along with other brassicas, mizuna contains glucosinolates, which may inhibit the development of certain cancers.

Mizuna 'Red Coral' (*Brassica juncea* 'Red Coral')

Mizuna seedlings have white stems and bright green cotyledons. The true leaf is attractive and serrated; it's known as one of the fastest and most productive microgreens to grow and is a staple in the microgreens and baby leaf markets. Germination is rapid and the crop usually has few disease problems. However, I've had crops rot after an initial successful burst of growing — I may have overwatered.

'Red Coral' grows with a blush of burgundy colour and looks most attractive. It has a mild, sweet, fresh mustard taste, and a wide range of uses: with salads, meats or grown longer for use in baby leaf salads. In my vegetable garden the deeply cut jagged leaves look beautiful; I cut side shoots for salads.

The flavour is hot and fresh . . . it's delicious.

Above: Mustard streaks.

Mustard

Mustard dates back over 5000 years and has been cultivated for both its seed and leaf. There are several plant species in the *Brassica* and *Sinapsis* genera. As well as the small seeds being used as a spice, they are ground to make mustard paste and pressed for oil. The mustard greens have also long been consumed.

As well as the following mustards, I have had great success with several types of mustard seed bought from a spice shop. As the seed was sold for cooking purposes the variety was not known; the label just says 'mustard' but it's delicious anyway! It packs a real punch. The flavours are hot and spicy, reminiscent of hot English mustard but not quite as 'nose clearing'.

Mustard streaks (*Brassica juncea*)

Mustard can also be grown as a gourmet vegetable in the garden. *Brassica juncea* is a herbaceous plant commonly known as mustard greens, Indian mustard, Chinese mustard and leaf mustard. It has numerous cultivars, many used in Chinese and Japanese cuisine, such as mizuna and gai choy.

The delicious combination of mustard and cress has been around for years for use in sandwiches and salads. Mustard streaks add a spiky texture and peppery taste to both.

I've let some of my mustard streaks microgreens grow for longer and they produce crisp, springy stems with a peppery bite. We used them in the Rice Paper Rolls on page 82 to add a stronger flavour and different texture to the more mild ingredients. It's great as a more mature plant to use as baby salad leaves too. Their strong, springy, upright stems are easy to cut and re-cut.

Mustard streaks are easy to grow. They're dependable in germination and yield. Definitely one to select if you choose to grow only a small repertoire of microgreens. The leaves look like finely cut mizuna. Sow and re-sow to have a supply of cutting stems say every two to three weeks for a year-round supply; they don't mind cold weather.

Mustard streaks are high in vitamins A and K.

Black mustard (*Brassica nigra*)

This mustard is very easy to grow as a microgreen, as are all the mustards. Mustards, including this one, like both seed-raising mix and pumice.

In the garden black mustard is an annual plant cultivated for its seeds, which are commonly used as spice. In Ethiopia it is cultivated as a vegetable; the shoots and leaves are consumed cooked and the seeds used as a spice.

Black mustard has been shown in studies to reduce the rate of colon, bladder and lung cancers. It has high levels of antioxidants such as sulphoraphane. Regular consumption of mustard microgreens enhances the body's biological barriers to cancer development.

I love it in salads with milder flavoured greens, or in wraps, even in scrambled eggs to add some zing.

I also grow it in the garden as a salad or stir-fry green. The plant itself can grow from 60 to 120 cm (2 to 4 feet) tall with racemes of small yellow flowers.

Black mustard is thought to be native to the southern Mediterranean region, and has been cultivated since ancient times. It has been speculated that black mustard is the seed mentioned by Jesus in Matthew 13:31–32.

Above and opposite: Mustard microgreens.

Parsley

Parsley is one of the world's best-known and most frequently used herbs, popular in Middle Eastern, European and American cooking. The two forms used are the curly leaf and the flat leaf or Italian. Parsley is rich in iron.

Italian parsley (*Petroselinum crispum* var. *neapolitanum*)

Microgreen Italian (flat leaf) parsley has a distinctive sweet/spicy parsley flavour and rich dark green leaves the shape of shamrock. As a full grown plant the leaves are a traditional ingredient in a bouquet garni.

As a microgreen, the seeds can have a patchy strike rate, and the plant is a slow grower. Soaking seeds in warm water for 24 hours before planting may help. But it is well worth the effort. Let it grow long enough to develop its true leaves before you cut. Cut as needed; there is no need to store.

It's lovely sprinkled on pasta, added to sandwich fillings, or as a garnish. Flat leaf parsley is preferred by many cooks these days because it has a strong but smoother flavour than the curly leaf form.

Peas

Widely favoured as a gourmet garnish, pea shoots have been available for a long time. The shoots are sweet, crunchy and taste like freshly podded peas or young snow peas — delicious. They have a long, crunchy stem that taste like snow pea pods. They may also be called sugar pea, sugar snap, snap peas, pea shoots, Oregon sugar pod or he lan do.

It is best to use untreated pea seed as any fungicide or other chemicals can be carried over to the harvestable portion of the seedling. Peas may be pre-soaked in warm water for 24 hours before sowing. Grow them at a high density: sprinkle seed over the soil or pumice in a full single layer and they will produce attractive, tall, straight pea shoots with a white blanched stem and fresh green leaves. Cover the seeds with soil and make sure that you don't expose them when watering.

Don't plant too many at once; do them in stages. Their flavour is better when they are about 5 cm (2 inches) high. If they've been allowed to grow too tall cut them high on the stem. Don't leave them growing too long, though, as the stems will become woody.

Peas are a cool weather crop; if you grow them in the summer keep them in the shade otherwise they can lose their colour and sweet taste. Their fresh spring flavour is a bonus in the winter months. They are one of the quickest and most versatile crops microgreen growers can produce, particularly indoors. Children love them, too.

Opposite: Italian parsley.

Above: Snow peas.

They can be harvested and stored in plastic containers or bags in the fridge but are better freshly cut.

Sprouted and microgreen beans and legumes such as peas are a good source of protein, carbohydrate and vitamin C. They also contain vitamin B1, iron, niacin, magnesium and zinc.

Watch out for bird thieves — they love peas. Sparrows took a liking to mine, zipping off the leaves and stealing the whole huge pea seed. Now I cover the pots with clear plastic shower hats. It must be confusing for the birds; I feed them from the same balcony and they think they can tuck into anything. Rodents apparently enjoy peas, too.

Unlike many other microgreens, peas will re-grow if the stems are not cut too low down at harvest. And to clean them, a quick rinse is all that's needed; there's no chance of soil being attached as they are picked well above the soil level. The tendrils tend to repel water, making them quick to dry.

Peas are thought to have originated in western Asia and derived from the wild pea. Cultivated by the Hebrews, Persians and Greeks, and later the Romans, peas are now found throughout most of the world. Evidence has been found of them as a cultivated plant at a Stone Age lake village site in Switzerland. They were regarded as a decadent luxury in the 1600s in Europe.

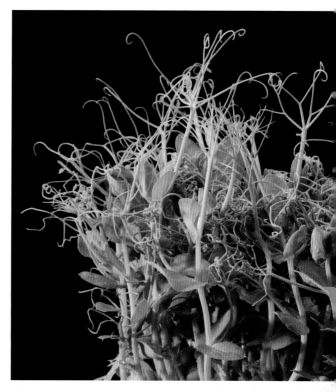

Above: Affilla® Cress, a cultivar of Pisum sativum *with attractive curling tendrils.*

Snow Pea (*Pisum sativum*)

Snow peas are delicious whole or chopped up and added to salads. Like 'Fiji Feathers' below they have the flavour of sweet, freshly podded peas. If your peas have got out of control and you have an excess growing too quickly, make them into a pea soup. The vibrant green colour will be stunning. Chopped and sprinkled on top of pea and ham soup they're fresh and complementary. They are especially delicious in the Rice Paper Rolls recipe on page 82 or in a mixed green salad. They can also add another texture and fresh flavour to stir-fries. Stir-fried alone they're good with some finely grated fresh ginger and a splash of rice wine.

Pea 'Fiji Feathers' (*Pisum sativum* 'Fiji Feathers')

The pea 'Fiji Feathers' has been bred to grow tendrils on young pea seedlings, giving a very attractive shoot with the flavour of sweet, freshly podded peas. Pea tendrils are the fine, feathered green feeler, which the plant uses to attach itself to climbing supports. 'Fiji Feathers' produces long tendrils and has less leaf than snow peas. Similar varieties with feathery tendrils can be found in various countries. Grow and harvest them as for snow peas. They give salads, cooked dishes and meats an exotic and interesting appearance.

Radish (*Raphanus sativus*)

Radish microgreens are among the easiest to grow, in both temperate and cooler climates, and they always perform. They're a fast and effortless grower like garden-grown radishes. They don't require any special attention. Being ready to pick at the cotyledon leaf stage rather than waiting for the real leaves to develop makes them quicker too.

There are numerous varieties available. Some microgreens have hints of reddish pink and vibrant purple leaves, such as radish sango. Others have gorgeous pink stems. Cut long stems to show the striking stem colour. Full sun will help achieve best stem colour and so will cooler temperatures. Because of the immediate and almost guaranteed success, they're a good one to start children on growing. I've had huge success with plain green radish.

When harvested at cotyledon stage they will remain tender and keep their vivid stem colour. If they are allowed to grow past that stage they will be woody and tough —throw them into stocks or soups then.

They're good as a colour spiker and add bite to mixed green salads. Good, too, in sandwiches, sprinkled on top of soups and stews, as a garnish, or to make an edible bed for cooked vegetables. Or try our vibrant Raw Energy Salad on page 85.

They are full of flavour and while emerging radish leaves are spicy some radish microgreens can be as hot and pungent as a mature radish root. Tender but crisp, they're not too fragile and are easy to wash. You'll find lots of seed hulls in the washing water. They are light and will float to the top. Scoop them out by hand and keep washing until there are none left.

Darker-coloured varieties are high in vitamins, minerals and antioxidants (see Chapter 4, Nutrition). They rank with broccoli and the other brassicas as a health-giving food.

Left: Radish sango.
Opposite: Daikon radish.

Humans have been eating radishes for ages. A large type of radish almost certainly dates back to prehistoric times in Europe. By about 10,000 BC in Asia people discovered that, at the right time of year, radishes and turnips put back into the ground would continue to grow. During the first millennium AD radish was a common root crop in Europe.

Daikon radish (*Raphanus sativus* var. *longipinnatus*)

Daikon is a large, white radish from east Asia. As a microgreen, it has crisp, long, white stems with soft green leaves; it is spicy and hot with quite an 'after-blast'. Like the other radishes it is easy and quick to grow and strong, and can be raised in either seed-raising mix or pumice.

The plant is full of vitamins, amino acids, antioxidants and minerals. A recent study by the Queensland Department of Primary Industries and Fisheries in Australia of the cancer-blocking potential of 22 brassicas rated radish, daikon and broccoli sprouts as the most powerful brassica-based anti-carcinogens, with the radish sprouts possibly outperforming broccoli sprouts. Daikon microgreens are good in salads, soups, wraps and sandwiches.

Rocket (Arugula) (*Eruca sativa*)

Rocket microgreens provide a sharp, piquant seasoning for salads. Their peppery bite and pungent flavour is also lovely to spike up sandwiches or even as a pizza topping. Rocket has gained popularity in modern cooking since the early 1990s.

They are easy and fast to grow, especially in cool weather; I had great success in autumn. Apparently, the seeds can germinate in temperatures as low as 4.4°C (40°F). The plant looks gorgeous growing as a microgreen — a cushion of grass green seedlings. Its quick germination and growth make it ideal for most people to grow.

Some patches can rot due to lack of air flow. Birds took a liking to mine; I covered the container to deter them, but that made the seedlings susceptible to rot. I think I overwatered, too, causing rotting patches.

Pumice is a good medium to grow it in; it can be tedious to wash if grown in soil. It has a mucilaginous seed, which makes it cling to the bottom of its cotyledons.

The greens are delicate to wash as the leaves and stems are fragile; this also makes it difficult to water from above. If leaves collapse, gently lift them back up.

Rocket has many vernacular names including arugula, roquette and rughetta. Native to the Mediterranean region, it was popular as a salad plant in Roman times, and may sometimes be heard referred to as Roman rocket. It was also used medicinally.

Opposite: Rocket (arugula).

Wheatgrass (*Triticum aestivum*)

Wheatgrass is the young grass of a common wheat plant. As a microgreen it has been around for years. Although classed as a microgreen, it is used in an entirely different way — to make a health-promoting juice.

Wheatgrass juice is abundant in vitamins, minerals, enzymes, protein and chlorophyll. It contains every amino acid, vitamin and mineral necessary for human nutrition, making it one of the few actual 'whole foods'.

Wheatgrass is so nutrient-rich that only 30 ml (less than 1/8 cup) of freshly squeezed wheatgrass juice is equivalent in nutritional value to 1 kg (2.2 lbs) of leafy green vegetables.

Kilo for kilo, it has more vitamin C than oranges and twice the vitamin A of carrots. However, this is only true when wheatgrass is grown on organic soil which has not been depleted of minerals.

Wheatgrass is believed to lower blood pressure and cholesterol levels, increase red blood cells, relieve blood sugar disorders such as diabetes, and aid in the prevention of some cancers.

It's easy to grow. Wheatgrass seed may be pre-soaked in warm water for 24 hours before sowing; I do this. Sow seed thickly and lightly cover with soil. Keep the seeds well watered.

Wheatgrass shoots are grown for longer than other shoots and for this reason they benefit from additions of dilute, well-balanced hydroponic nutrient because food reserves in the wheat grain are exhausted long before the wheatgrass is harvested. Dilute nutrient can be applied daily, once germination has occurred. Use of hydroponic nutrients that contain minerals beneficial to human health (such as selenium and chromium) can give wheatgrass, which is grown for a longer time, a real boost in mineral content.

Reasonably strong natural light also helps boost vitamin and chlorophyll content in densely grown wheatgrass.

On my first attempt, the sparrows found mine and pecked right through the plastic shower hat cover.

To harvest, cut the tops off after stems are about 20 to 25 cm (8 to 10 inches) high. Liquidize in a blender and drink 5 to 10 ml (1 to 2 teaspoons) per day washed down with two glasses of water, preferably at mealtimes.

The juice can be stored in the fridge for a week or frozen/freeze dried without any loss of goodness.

Opposite: Wheatgrass.

6

children growing microgreens

'Plant a radish; get a radish, never any doubt. That's why I love vegetables; you know what they're about!'
— *Tom Jones and Harvey Schmidt*

- Fast growing — quick reward
- Cute containers
- Now . . . the eating

Fast growing — quick reward

Microgreens are an ideal way to teach children how to raise and eat fresh, leafy vegetables, and to learn that they come from the earth, not the shop. Because microgreens grow quickly they give instant satisfaction for children's effort and hold interest — no time for boredom and giving up. Choose fast-growing seeds that are generally fail-proof, such as radish, kale or peas.

As an introduction, choose small, interesting containers (see below) for children and a variety of seeds. It's a sure-fire way to keep kids' attention. Peas are good to start with. The variety 'Fiji Feathers' and similar varieties have long, wiry tendrils that look fascinating, and the whole lot can be eaten. They are sweet, too, and they grow exuberantly (see page 69). Radishes are also fast, easy growers but their flavour may be a bit spicy for novice palettes.

Cute containers

See-through plastic containers are good for kids, especially if you use pumice as the growing medium because the roots can be seen through the sides. Covering with towels rather than soil allows kids to sneak a peak at growing seeds and watch them develop roots and shoots and become plants. Children love small, amusing, quirky, fun containers. Some possibilities are listed overleaf.

- Recycled food cans may be painted by children and they hold small quantities. Hammer a couple of small holes with a nail in the bottom for drainage.
- Try using a whole cardboard egg tray and planting something different in each hole. Some egg cartons are porous, too, so will not become waterlogged. Sit them on a sturdy tray to drain into. The roots will start to invade the soft material of the carton.
- Poppy enjoyed planting seed in pumice inside small Asian steam baskets, another fun container. It has a slatted bottom for drainage.
- Small plastic containers that will fit into watertight bowls such the 'La Salade' bowl on page 104.
- A vintage enamel colander works well as it has plenty of drainage and looks quirky. We grew wheatgrass in ours but any micro would be suitable.
- Individual salad bowls are just right for a small plastic punnet of greens and they are a manageable size for children.
- Cardboard noodle boxes are just the right size for one of the standard plastic flower pots that nurseries and plant centres use. Put some plastic in the bottom to save the cardboard box base from becoming soggy.
- Save tiny food cans or plastic pottles that will fit inside things like tea cups. It's easy to cut the top off plastic if it's too tall. We grew red cabbage for our cabbage-style cup, radish for our tiny white Asian cup and cress for our Pooh Bear cup (that crop was for the girls' caged budgie, too).
- The sundae glasses were an op-shop bargain and have tiny holders of mustard growing in them and a few nasturtium leaves to hide the commercial labels.
- We carefully sliced the tops off eggs high up on the egg (before poaching) so that we had room for some soil mix, pierced a hole in the bottom of the egg for drainage, and grew all sorts of micros. They need regular watering as they do not hold much soil and micros are ultra thirsty. The girls had fun drawing faces on the egg shells, too.
- The tiny plastic scoops that are included inside cartons of soap powder are fun for tiny micro samples — just enough harvest for a sandwich each. Punch a split in the bottom. They need regular watering as they hold only a small amount of soil.

Now . . . the eating

Once the microgreens are ready to harvest, children can experiment with how they would like to consume them. The Rice Paper Rolls on page 82 are great for kids and they can have a sticky go themselves at making the rolls.

Corn and Feta Fritters (page 93) are also fun to make and the kids can use cookie cutter shapes to pour the batter into. Serve with a sweet chilli sauce.

Add a handful of microgreens to sandwiches, pita pockets, wraps or tacos along with other fillings. A bunch in a hamburger works well, too.

Top left: The children have used plastic drink bottles with their bases cut off to create mini-glasshouses over tin-can planters for microgreens.
Top right: Strawberries and mustard microgreens. The mustard micros have been planted in tiny plastic bowls that fit inside sundae glasses with nasturtium leaves as decoration.
Above: Mustard microgreens in a line-up of egg shells in an egg carton.

7

recipes

'You have to eat to cook. You can't be a good cook and be a non-eater.
I think eating is the secret to good cooking.'
— *Julia Child*

- Rice Paper Rolls
- Raw Energy Salad
- Spicy Asian Microgreen Salad
- Stuffed Mushrooms
- Dressings and Dips
- Turkish Rolls with Feta and Fennel Spread
- Asian Minced Chicken Salad
- Corn, Feta Cheese and Microgreen Fritters
- Pear, Avocado and Microgreen Salad
- Microgreen, Bean and Winter Green Gratin
- Chard and Microgreen Frittata
- Strawberries with Basil Microgreens

Raw, freshly cut microgreens are my preference rather than cooking them. They are highly flavoured and tender as well as colourful. Along with being fun to grow, microgreens are enjoyable to eat. And their nutritional potency is a bonus.

They're wonderful added to a salad, as a salad themselves or as a raw garnish to enhance a dish or just decoration on a nibbles platter.

Sometimes I've had just one type of lettuce: I tear it up into a salad bowl and throw in handfuls of rinsed micros of different varieties, a few olives, capers and pink ginger from the fridge. I love mint and cress and always have some growing full size on my balcony; I tear a little of those leaves in and, hey presto, I have an interesting salad.

Ordinary green mustard is so prolific; I can pull a ring of outer sprigs out and still have a generous mop-top for several more helpings.

Microgreens are also useful raw in sandwiches, wraps, snacks, burgers, stuffings and more. When I have volume I use them in cooked dishes.
Mustard and mizuna spike up bland greens in, say, a cooked flan. Some are good added to a stir-fry but they do tend to get lost visually. A few stirred into scrambled eggs at the last minute works well. I'll never stop experimenting with microgreens.

Rice Paper Rolls

12 rounds rice paper

FILLING
1 cup pea shoots microgreens
1 cup mustard streaks microgreens
½ cup pickled ginger slices, cut in slivers
2 large carrots, cut in fine long slivers
2 zucchini, unpeeled, slivered lengthwise
2 green onions, finely sliced lengthways
1 large yellow capsicum (bell pepper/sweet pepper), finely sliced
  lengthways
Calendula, evening primrose and borage petals

- Have a clean damp tea towel ready.
- Dip one rice paper wrapper at a time in warm water until just beginning to soften; gently shake off water; cover with towel to keep damp and soften for about a minute.
- Place a selection of all the vegetables on a softened rice paper round.
- Roll up tightly, placing petals on final round so they look colourful.
- Keep in the fridge under a damp tea towel until ready to serve.
- Serves 6.

Cooked shrimps or shredded chicken could be added to this mix. Try them with a Chilli Dip (see page 89).

Opposite: Rice Paper Rolls.

Raw Energy Salad

¼ cup pumpkin seeds
¼ cup sunflower seeds
2 teaspoons cumin seeds
1½ cups microgreens — red cabbage, radish and purple basil
   are good
1 raw beetroot, peeled and grated
1 large carrot, grated
¼ red cabbage, finely shredded
½ red capsicum (bell pepper/sweet pepper), finely sliced
½ red onion, finely sliced
1 teaspoon black sesame seeds
1 cup cooked quinoa (red if possible)

- Combine pumpkin seeds, sunflower seeds and cumin seeds.
- Lightly toast in a frying pan over a medium heat, stirring continuously.
- Combine cooled seeds with all other ingredients.
- Drizzle Pomegranate Dressing (see page 89) over the salad and serve.
- Serves 6.

Spicy Asian Microgreen Salad

4 teaspoons (20 ml) lemon juice
½ teaspoon finely sliced chilli
2 teaspoons (10 ml) fish sauce
1 teaspoon sugar
2 teaspoons fried shallots
2 teaspoons fried garlic
1 cup microgreens
½ cup cooked shrimps
Fennel slices
4 teaspoons (20 ml) coconut cream

- Mix the lemon juice, chilli, fish sauce, sugar, fried shallots, fried garlic and fold in the microgreens.
- Garnish with shrimps, fennel slices and coconut cream.
- Sprinkle a few microgreens on top.
- Serves 2.

Opposite: Raw Energy Salad.

Stuffed Mushrooms

2 cloves garlic, chopped
1 small red onion, finely chopped
6 large flat mushrooms
2 slices grainy bread, crumbed
½ cup toasted sunflower seeds
½ cup grated cheddar cheese
Handful of microgreens
Salt and ground pepper to taste
2 tablespoons olive oil

- Lightly sauté the garlic and onion.
- Cut as much of the stalk as possible from the mushrooms. Chop stalk finely.
- Mix all ingredients together.
- Wet hands and gather enough stuffing for one mushroom; squeeze to compact it.
- Press firmly on to the top of each mushroom, covering all the gills.
- Bake on a flat oven dish at 180°C (350 °F) for 15 minutes. If wished, grill lightly to brown the tops.
- Serve with a generous garnish of fresh microgreens and a drizzle of oil.
- Serves 3.

Additional optional ingredients could be capers, a couple of anchovy fillets finely sliced, olives chopped, pickled gherkins finely sliced and chillies.

Opposite: Stuffed Mushrooms with preserved green figs.

Dressings and Dips

Garam Masala Dressing

This dressing, a blend of sweet and hot spices, is lovely with a salad containing fruit such as Asian pears and microgreens (see page 93).

½ cup sugar
2 cups (500 ml) water
1 piece cinnamon stick (5 cm/2 inches long)
2 pieces fresh ginger, smashed (2.5 x 0.5 cm/1 x ¼ inch)
2 teaspoons green or white cardamom pods, lightly crushed
2 teaspoons coriander seeds, lightly crushed
10 whole black peppercorns, lightly crushed
¼ teaspoon dried hot red pepper flakes

- Melt sugar and water, add all spices.
- Cool.
- Serve with your salad of choice.

Curry Vinaigrette

4 teaspoons curry powder
2 teaspoons (10 ml) water
½ cup (125 ml) oil
2 tablespoons (10 ml) cider vinegar
½ teaspoon minced garlic
Scant ½ teaspoon salt
¼ teaspoon black pepper
6 cups microgreens

- Stir together curry powder and water in a small bowl to make a paste. Let stand 5 minutes, and then stir in oil and let stand, stirring occasionally for an hour.
- Pour curry oil through a papertowel-lined sieve into a small cup, discarding solids.
- Combine vinegar, garlic, salt and pepper, then add curry oil, whisking until combined.
- Pour over microgreens. Gently combine.

Above: Chilli Dip.

Chilli Dip

> 2 teaspoons chilli
> 1½ tablespoons ginger
> 3 tablespoons (40 ml) lime or lemon juice
> 4 teaspoons (20 ml) fish sauce
> 3 tablespoons (40 ml) honey (runny)
> 1½ tablespoons fresh coriander, chopped
> 1½ tablespoons black sesame seeds
> 1½ tablespoons (20 ml) sesame oil

- Pound chilli and ginger in pestle and mortar for 10 minutes until they form a paste.
- Add all other ingredients except oil.
- Add oil gently and mix together.
- Serve in a dipping bowl with rice paper rolls.

Pomegranate Dressing

> 4 teaspoons (20 ml) pomegranate molasses or paste
> Juice and finely grated zest of 1 orange
> 4 tablespoons (50 ml) olive oil
> Sea salt and finely ground black pepper
> 1 tablespoon finely chopped mint

- Mix all together.

Turkish Rolls with Feta and Fennel Spread

4 square sheets of Turkish wraps
3 cups microgreens, loosely packed
½ cup pickled baby ginger slices, chopped
1 pickled lemon peel, finely sliced
2 cups (approx. 8 oz/250 g) cooked chicken
2 capsicums (bell peppers/sweet peppers), finely sliced
Ground black pepper

- On each Turkish wrap spread a thin layer of Feta and Fennel Spread.
- On top sprinkle mixed microgreens, chopped baby ginger, finely sliced pickled lemon peel, pieces of cooked chicken, capsicums and ground black pepper.
- Roll up tightly.
- Slice into 5 cm (2 inch) lengths.
- Serve upright so that guests can see the filling. Serves 4–8.

Feta and Fennel Spread

1 tablespoon fennel seeds
1 cup (250 g) soft, creamy feta cheese
Water

- Toast fennel seeds in a heavy dry frying pan over a medium heat until they begin to pop.
- Crush with a pestle and mortar or on a chopping board with a rolling pin.
- Mix with the feta in a food processor, or mash feta with a fork and add fennel. Add water if necessary to make a smooth creamy texture. Refrigerate.

Asian Minced Chicken Salad

1 tablespoon rice
2 teaspoons (10 ml) olive oil
14 oz (400 g) chicken mince
2 tablespoons (25 ml) fish sauce
1 stem lemon grass, white part only, finely chopped
6 tablespoons (80 ml) chicken stock
3 tablespoons (40 ml) lime juice
4 green onions, finely sliced diagonally
4 shallots or red onion, sliced
3 tablespoons coriander leaves, finely chopped
3 tablespoons mint, finely chopped
Dash of cayenne pepper (optional)
1 cup microgreens
3 tablespoons chopped, roasted, unsalted peanuts
1 small fresh red chilli, sliced to garnish
Lime wedges to serve

- Heat a frying pan and dry fry rice over a low heat for three minutes, or until golden. Grind in a pestle and mortar to a fine powder.
- Heat a pan or wok over medium heat. Add the oil, then chicken mince and cook for 4 minutes or until it changes colour. Break up the lumps.
- Add the fish sauce, lemon grass and stock and cook for a further 10 minutes. Cool.
- Add lime juice, green onions, shallots, coriander, mint, cayenne pepper (if using) and ground rice. Mix well.
- Arrange cleaned microgreens on a serving platter (you could add some sliced lettuce as well if wished). Top with chicken salad. Sprinkle with nuts and chilli and serve with lime wedges.
- Serves 4–6.

This dish (often called Larb Gai) is usually served on a bed of shredded lettuce or cabbage; microgreens make a fresh change.

Corn, Feta Cheese and Microgreen Fritters

BATTER
1 cup flour
1 tablespoon baking powder
1 teaspoon salt
Freshly ground black pepper
2 eggs
½ cup (125 ml) soda water

OTHER INGREDIENTS
2 cups whole corn kernels
½ cup (125 g) crumbled feta cheese
1 cup microgreens, mixed or one variety

- Sift dry ingredients
- Mix all the batter ingredients until smooth.
- Add corn and feta cheese, and stir, add microgreens last, stir.
- Stand mix for 10 minutes.
- Cook spoonfuls in a small amount of oil in a pan over medium heat until golden on both sides.
- Serve with a chutney of your choice and a microgreen salad.
- Makes approximately 12 fritters.

Pear, Avocado and Microgreen Salad

2 nashi pears (Asian pears)
2 avocados
¼ cup (60 ml) freshly squeezed lemon juice
4 cups microgreens of your choice
½ cup sunflower seeds
Garam Masala Dressing from page 88

- Peel and slice pears and avocados. Cover with lemon juice.
- Add microgreens and sunflower seeds.
- Add Garam Masala Dressing.
- Toss gently and serve. Serves 4.

Opposite: Corn, Feta Cheese and Microgreen Fritters.

Microgreen, Bean and Winter Green Gratin

1 cup dry white beans (cannellini are good)
Bouquet garni
½ teaspoon salt
1 large bunch winter greens, e.g. beet, mustard, sorrel, chard
2 cloves garlic, finely chopped
2 tablespoons (25 ml) olive oil
1 cup peeled, seeded and chopped tomatoes (canned are fine)
½ cup chopped ham
2 cups microgreens (broccoli, kale, red cabbage,
   mustard and rocket/arugula are good)
½ cup (125 ml) chicken stock
1 cup fresh breadcrumbs
4 tablespoons (50 ml) olive oil
¼ teaspoon salt

- Soak the beans overnight. Drain, put into a large pot with 3 cups water, and the bouquet garni. Simmer for 45 minutes and salt the water (½ teaspoon). Continue cooking for another 15 minutes. There won't be much liquid left in the pot — about ½ cup.
- Wash winter greens, remove stalks and cut leaves in ribbon strips.
- Sauté the garlic in oil and then add the greens. Cook for about 7 minutes.
- Add the beans and their cooking liquid, the tomatoes, ham and the microgreens.
- Add chicken stock in stages if the mixture seems dry.
- Oil a 25 cm (10 inch) gratin dish and spoon the mixture in. Mix the breadcrumbs with the remaining 4 tablespoons of oil and ¼ teaspoon salt. Spread over the top of the base mixture.
- Bake in a 175°C (350°F) oven for 40 to 50 minutes.
- Serves 4–6.

Lovely served with a crunchy green salad with some shavings of fresh fennel bulb.

Chard and Microgreen Frittata

1 clove garlic
2 tablespoons (25 ml) virgin olive oil
2 cups ruby chard, stems removed, leaves cut in
    1 cm (½ inch approx.) strips
1 cup microgreens of your choice
6 large eggs
¼ teaspoon sea salt
¼ cup finely grated parmesan
Generous pinch hot paprika

- Place garlic and 1 tablespoon of the oil in a 24 cm (9½ inch) skillet over medium heat and cook until garlic begins to brown, about 3 minutes.
- Add the chard, stir, cover and cook until it has wilted and turned dark green (about 25 minutes), stirring occasionally to be sure it doesn't stick to the bottom of pan. Add microgreens and gently stir.
- In a large bowl, whisk eggs, salt, parmesan and paprika until just broken up. Preheat grill.
- Add remaining oil to the vegetables, stir, and make sure it doesn't stick to the bottom of the pan. Pour the eggs over the chard and let them cook until they are set on the bottom, which will take 4 to 5 minutes. Let eggs set except for about 0.5 cm (¼ inch) on the top.
- Remove pan from heat and place 12.5 cm (5 inches) from the grill. Cook (1 to 2 minutes) until the top is just set and there is no uncooked egg. Don't overcook.
- Remove from heat and place the serving platter on top of pan. Invert pan so frittata falls onto platter. Cool to room temperature before serving.
- Serves 4.

Strawberries with Basil Microgreens

Strawberries and basil are a fresh combination. Try this simple summer dessert.

2 tablespoons sugar
1 cup strawberries quartered or halved depending on size
Fresh juice of one orange
Fresh juice and pulp of 4 passionfruit
½ a handful of basil microgreens

- Sprinkle sugar over cut strawberries.
- Toss strawberries and sugar gently in orange and passionfruit juices.
- Stand for 15 minutes.
- Toss in basil microgreens, keeping a few pristine sprigs for the top.
- Squeeze passionfruit pulp over strawberries. Serve in glasses.
- Serves 3–4.

Opposite and above: Strawberries with Basil Microgreens.

resources

For seeds, supplies, information and more.

Seed Suppliers

Chiltern Seeds, www.chilternseeds.co.uk
D. T. Browns, www.dtbrownseeds.co.uk
Delfland Nurseries, www.rocketgardens.co.uk
Dobies, www.dobies.co.uk
Marshalls Seeds, www.marshalls-seeds.co.uk
Mr. Fothergill's, www.mr-fothergills.co.uk
Nicky's Nursery, www.nickys-nursery.co.uk
Suffolk Herbs, www.suffolkherbs.com
Suttons Seeds, www.suttons.co.uk
The Heritage Seed Library, www.gardenorganic.org.uk
The Organic Gardening Catalogue, www.organiccatalog.com
The Real Seed Company, www.realseeds.co.uk
Thomas Etty, www.thomasetty.co.uk
Unwins, www.unwins.co.uk
Victoriana Nursery Gardens www.victoriananursery.co.uk

Useful websites

www.biodynamic.org.uk
www.rhs.org.uk
www.seedtoplate.co.uk
www.soilassociation.org
www.fionnahill.com

Book

Franks, Eric and Jasmine Richardson, *Microgreens: a guide to growing nutrient-packed greens*, Gibbs Smith, 2009.

Acknowledgements

With many thanks to:
- Brian O'Flaherty
- Claire Bennett
- Diana Anderson
- Dorothy Motoi
- Gerard and Barbara Martin, Kings Seeds
- Grant Allen
- Grey Lynn Community Gardens

- Jed Fahey, Johns Hopkins University
- Kings Seeds
- Koppert Cress
- Linda Hallinan
- Mike O'Donnell
- *New Zealand Gardener* magazine
- Peter Sharp
- Poppy Constantine
- Ray Dwyer
- Rob Baan and Jan Van Berkel, Koppert Cress
- Sally Tagg
- Shirley Anderson
- Sierra O'Donnell
- Tallulah O'Donnell
- Tim O'Hare, Gatton Research Station
- Tracey Borgfeldt
- Alice Bell

Photo credits

Photographs by the author unless credited otherwise below.

Francine Cameron
www.francinephotography.co.nz
page 25, 67
Koppert Cress pages 47, 65, 69
Mike O'Donnell pages 6, 20 (right), 22 (left), 76, 79 (top right)
Sally Tagg www.sallytagg.co.nz
pages 5, 14 (both), 49 (right), 80, 83, 84, 87, 89, 92, 96, 97, 107

Photograph stylist
Fionna Hill

Glossary

Brassicas
Members of the Brassica plant genus in the mustard family Brassicaceae, such as broccoli, cabbage, kale, mustard, radish.

Compounds
A compound is a substance made from two or more elements.

Cotyledons
'Seed leaves' that begins as part of the embryo within the seed of a plant. In dicotyledonous plants they produce two kidney-shaped 'seed' leaves, the first leaves to appear. True leaves, by contrast, develop from the plant stem.

Cruciferous vegetables
Or 'crucifers'; members of the mustard family Brassicaceae, also known as Cruciferae, such as broccoli, cabbage, kale, mustard, radish, cress.

Diindolylmethane
A phytonutrient and plant indole (crystalline compound) found in cruciferous vegetables including broccoli, Brussels sprouts, cabbage, cauliflower and kale.

Flavonoids
Any of a large group of water-soluble plant pigments, including the anthocyanins, that are beneficial to health.

Glucosinolate
Substances occurring widely in plants of the genus Brassica, broccoli, cabbage, kale, mustard, radish. They are what give some brassicas their bitter flavour.

Lignans
A lignan is a phytochemical (plant-based substance) that can act like human oestrogen.

Omega-3
Omega-3 fatty acids are a type of unsaturated fat found in fish and plants.

Microgreen
Plants raised from seed that are larger than sprouts and smaller than 'baby' salad greens (the small leafy greens, edible flowers and herbs that are popular salad ingredients). Microgreens have produced at least two 'true' leaves after the cotyledons appear. Some are eaten at the cotyledon stage.

Pathogen
An infectious agent, such as bacteria and viruses, that causes disease or illness to its host.

Phytochemicals
Phytochemicals, or phytonutrients, are chemical compounds such as beta-carotene that occur naturally in plants.

Phytoestrogens
Phytoestrogens (also known as isoflavones) are a group of chemicals found in plants that can act like the hormone oestrogen. They are commonly found in beans (legumes), soy beans, cereal brans, flaxseeds, alfalfa and clover.

Phytonutrients
Phytochemicals, or phytonutrients, are chemical compounds such as beta-carotene that occur naturally in plants.

Sulphoraphane/Sulforaphane
An isothiocyanate phytochemical or 'nutriceutical' in cruciferous vegetables, such as broccoli, cabbage, kale, mustard, radish and cress.

Weights and measures: imperial equivalents

Length

Inches	Centimetres
¼	= 0.5
½	= 1.0
¾	= 2.0
1	= 2.5
2	= 5.0
3	= 8.0
4	= 10.0
6	= 15.0
8	= 20.0
10	= 25.0
12	= 30.0

Weights

Metric — Imperial	
15 g	= ½ oz
30 g	= 1 oz
60 g	= 2 oz
90 g	= 3 oz
125 g	= 4 oz (¼ lb)
250 g	= 8 oz (½ lb)
375 g	= 12 oz (¾ lb)
500 g (0.5 kg)	= 16 oz (1 lb)

Liquid measures

Teaspoon	Millilitres
¼ t	= 1.25 ml
½ t	= 2.5 ml
1 t	= 5 ml

Tablespoon	Millilitres
1 T	= 15 ml

Cup	Millilitres
¼ cup	= 62.5 ml
⅓ cup	= 83 ml
½ cup	= 125 ml
1 cup	= 250 ml

Pint	Millilitres
1 pint	= 570 ml
1¾ pint	= 1000 ml (1 litre)

Oven temperatures (guide only)

°F	°C
200	100
250	120
300	150
350	180
400	200
425	220
450	230
475	250

Index

Previous page: An old enamel colander is fun to grow microgreens (in this case wheatgrass) in, as it has built-in drainage. It needs to be placed on a saucer.
Opposite: Kale in a plastic container with drainage holes set inside a watertight ceramic bowl.

About the author

Fionna Hill is a high profile New Zealand floral designer. London-trained and experienced, she has run her own floral design business including floristry, floral workshops, function decorating and retail. She contributes to lifestyle and garden magazines on this subject, as well as general gardening, floral design, crafts and travel writing.

Fionna has been growing and eating microgreens for herself and her friends for several years. As well as microgreens being fresh and having sparkling flavours, she appreciates their nutritional properties and their popularity with children.

She has always used vegetables decoratively in her floral designs and has now turned her attention to growing them to eat. Living in a high-rise apartment, she values being able to grow organic vegetables in a community garden and sharing the knowledge of the inspirational 'garden gang'.

This is her fourth book. *Country Style Flowers* was an international success selling in Europe, the United Kingdom, the United States of America, and South Africa. She shared the writing of *Celebrations* with a food writer and contributed the floral designs for *The Christmas Book*, another international success.

Fionna lives in Auckland, New Zealand. www.fionnahill.com